Shall We Dance?

BALLET

by Wendy Hinote Lanier

FOCUS READERS

www.focusreaders.com

Focus Readers is distributed by North Star Editions:
sales@northstareditions.com | 888-417-0195

Produced for Focus Readers by Red Line Editorial.

Photographs ©: adriaticfoto/Shutterstock Images, cover, 1; Igor Bulgarin/Shutterstock Images, 4–5, 26; Photo12/Archives Snark/Alamy, 7; mcpix/iStockphoto, 8; Milkos/iStockphoto, 10–11, 18, 29; mavkate/iStockphoto, 12; Antonio Diaz/Shutterstock Images, 14–15; Photobac/Shutterstock Images, 17; oleg66/iStockphoto, 21; Sergey Petrov/Shutterstock Images, 22–23; Creatista/Shutterstock Images, 25

ISBN
978-1-63517-271-3 (hardcover)
978-1-63517-336-9 (paperback)
978-1-63517-466-3 (ebook pdf)
978-1-63517-401-4 (hosted ebook)

Library of Congress Control Number: 2017935124

Printed in the United States of America
Mankato, MN
June, 2017

About the Author

Wendy Hinote Lanier is a native Texan and former elementary teacher who writes and speaks for children and adults on a variety of topics. She is the author of more than 20 books for children and young people. Some of her favorite people are dogs.

TABLE OF CONTENTS

CHAPTER 1

A STORY IN A DANCE

The orchestra begins to play. The curtains rise. Then an elegant ballet dancer appears. She glides across the stage. Her twirls are graceful and beautiful. As she performs, she tells a story.

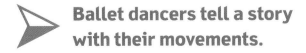

Ballet dancers tell a story with their movements.

The audience members watch in amazement.

A ballet involves more than just dancing. It also combines story and **mime**. People have loved ballet for centuries.

Ballet began in Italy in the late 1400s. By the 1600s, ballet became popular with the kings and queens of France. A French king started the first ballet school in 1669. This is why ballet terms are in French.

 An illustration shows a court ballet in Paris in the late 1600s.

The first ballet dancers were mostly men and boys. **Court** dress did not allow women to move freely.

 A teacher leads a ballet class.

And women were not supposed to show their feet and legs in public. The first female ballet dancers did not appear until the late 1600s. People's tastes started to change in the late 1700s. Female dancers became the stars of the show.

Today, ballet is taught and performed around the world. Many people enjoy going to ballet shows. But you can do more than simply watch ballet. You can also take a class and learn for yourself.

DANCE TIP

Ballet requires strength and stamina. Running and biking help improve these things.

CHAPTER 2

WHAT TO WEAR

Ballet clothes should fit close to your body. They also must allow you to move freely. When practicing, girls usually wear **leotards** and tights. Boys wear T-shirts and tights.

Tights help show a ballerina's form.

Pointe shoes have a hard toe box that allows dancers to stay high on their toes.

Ballet shoes are made of soft leather. They are tight at first. But they stretch over time. One or two pieces of elastic are sewn across the top. The elastic keeps the shoes in place. Drawstrings help, too.

Ballerinas sometimes wear pointe shoes. These shoes help ballerinas dance on their tiptoes. This is called dancing en pointe.

Performance ballet clothes are similar to practice clothes. Costumes help identify the characters in the ballet. Ballerinas often wear layered skirts called tutus.

DANCE TIP

Tie the drawstrings on your ballet shoes tight. Make a bow. Then tuck the bow into the front of your shoe. This keeps the bow out of sight.

CHAPTER 3

GETTING STARTED

Ballet is based on five basic steps. These steps are also known as positions. In each position, the legs turn out from the hip. All other ballet steps begin or end with one of the five positions.

A ballet teacher demonstrates first position.

Advanced dancers can learn more complicated steps.

Ballet classes usually start with **barre** (bar) exercises. These exercises help dancers warm up. Dancers then move to the center of the floor. There they learn new steps. They also practice their jumps and traveling steps.

DANCE TIP

To avoid injury, warm up with stretching exercises before dancing.

 Ballerinas practice en pointe.

Ballet dancers create a story with their dance. They use **gestures** and body language. This helps show conversation. Dancers also practice complicated moves en pointe. They do jumps and other moves.

 A ballerina performs an arabesque.

An arabesque (ar-uh-*besk*) is
done on one leg. Stretch your other
leg behind you. One arm reaches

forward. The other reaches back.
A pirouette (pir-oo-*et*) is another
common ballet move. In this move,
the dancer spins on one leg.

The dancing combines with the
music and costumes. All together
this creates a magical experience
for the audience.

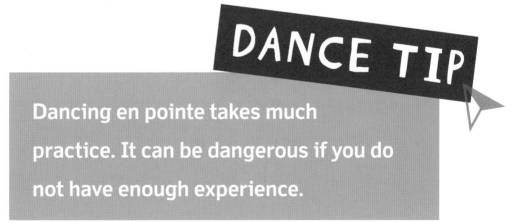

DANCE TIP

Dancing en pointe takes much practice. It can be dangerous if you do not have enough experience.

ROND DE JAMBE

A rond de jambe (rawn duh *zhanb*) is a half circle made with one leg. The other leg stays fixed. The move begins in first position. Your heels are together with your feet turned out.

1. Plant one foot firmly.
2. Brush the other foot forward with your toe pointed.
3. Keep your toe pointed. Move your leg from the front to the side and then to the back.
4. Complete the move by closing in first position. Keep your toe on the floor through the entire move.

Ballerinas practice doing a rond de jambe.

CHAPTER 4

ON WITH THE SHOW!

Most ballet dancers perform just for fun. The best dancers can become professionals. Getting to the top level can be difficult, though. First, dancers have to be accepted into a dance company.

Professional ballet companies often use fancy costumes.

They are usually chosen by an **audition**. Everyone begins by dancing with a large group. But with hard work, dancers can become soloists or **principals**.

Most countries have a ballet company. Many big cities do, too. Some companies perform in their own theater. Others travel and perform around the world.

A ballet company includes many people. There is a director. There is a **choreographer**. There is a set

 Ballet is a great way to spend time with your friends.

designer. And, of course, there are

the dancers.

 Ballet dancers perform *The Nutcracker*.

Today there are different styles of ballet. Some ballets are classic. Newer styles might use upbeat music. Dancers have more freedom in their movements. Their costumes might be funkier, too. But either way, an evening at the ballet is an unforgettable experience.

DANCE TIP

Proper alignment is important in ballet. It helps you move easily and efficiently. Imagine being pulled up by a straight line through the center of your body.

FOCUS ON
BALLET

Write your answers on a separate piece of paper.

1. Write a sentence that describes the key ideas from Chapter 1.

2. Do you think anyone can do ballet? Why or why not?

3. All ballet steps begin or end with a basic position. How many positions are there?
   A. two
   B. five
   C. nine

4. What might happen if you try to dance en pointe before you are ready?
   A. The height will make you dizzy.
   B. You might hurt your feet, legs, or back.
   C. You will make the other dancers look bad.

5. What does **conversation** mean in this book?

Ballet dancers create a story with their dance. They use gestures and body language. This helps show **conversation**.

    A. communication

    B. anger

    C. surprise

6. What does **elegant** mean in this book?

Then an **elegant** *ballet dancer appears. She glides across the stage. Her twirls are graceful and beautiful.*

    A. strong and sturdy

    B. fast moving

    C. pleasing to watch

Answer key on page 32.

GLOSSARY

audition
A short performance to test a performer's ability.

barre
A horizontal wooden bar attached to the wall that dancers use for support while they exercise.

choreographer
A person who creates dance routines.

court
The family, advisers, and other people close to a king or queen.

gestures
Movements of one's body to express an idea.

leotards
Formfitting one-piece clothes usually worn by dancers.

mime
An acting technique made up of gestures, movement, and facial expressions performed without speech.

principals
The highest-ranking dancers in a company.

stamina
The ability to continue working for a long time.

TO LEARN MORE

BOOKS

Copeland, Misty. *Life in Motion: An Unlikely Ballerina.* Young Readers ed. New York: Aladdin, 2016.

Hackett, Jane. *How to . . . Ballet: A Step-by-Step Guide to the Secrets of Ballet.* New York: DK, 2011.

Miles, Lisa. *Ballet Spectacular: A Young Ballet Lover's Guide and an Insight into a Magical World.* Hauppauge, NY: Barron's, 2015.

NOTE TO EDUCATORS

Visit **www.focusreaders.com** to find lesson plans, activities, links, and other resources related to this title.

INDEX

Answer Key: 1. Answers will vary; **2.** Answers will vary; **3.** B; **4.** B; **5.** A; **6.** C